The Appalachian

Erinn Banting

Weigl

CALGARY
www.weigl.ca

Published by Weigl Educational Publishers Limited
6325 – 10 Street SE
Calgary, Alberta, Canada
T2H 2Z9

Web site: www.weigl.ca

Library and Archives Canada Cataloguing in Publication

Banting, Erinn, 1976-
         The Appalachian / Erinn Banting.
(Canadian geographic regions)
Includes index.
ISBN 1-55388-140-0 (bound).--ISBN 1-55388-147-8 (pbk.)
         1. Atlantic Provinces--Geography--Textbooks.   2. Gaspé Peninsula
(Québec)--Geography--Textbooks.   3. Appalachian Region--Geography-
Textbooks. I. Title. II. Series.
FC2005.B35 2005   917.15   C2005-904573-6

Printed in the United States of America
2 3 4 5 6 7 8 9 0   09 08 07

CREDITS: Every reasonable effort has been made to trace ownership and to obtain permission to reprint copyright material. The publishers would be pleased to have any errors or omissions brought to their attention so that they may be corrected in subsequent printings.

COVER: The Mi'kmaq called Prince Edward Island *Epekwitk*, which means "resting on the waves."

Cover: Walter Bibikow/Taxi/Getty Images (front), John Warden/Stone/Getty Images (back);
Clipart.com: page 17; **European Space Agency:** page 41 (ESA/MERIS); **Getty Images:** pages 3 (Grant Faint/The Image Bank), 4L (Steve Bly/The Image Bank), 4ML (Paul Nicklen/National Geographic), 4MR (Philip & Karen Smith/Stone), 4R (Francesca York/Dorling Kindersley), 5L (Raymond K. Gehman/National Geographic), 5M (John Dunn/National Geographic), 5R (Ed Simpson/Stone), 6 (Tony Sweet/Digital Vision), 7 (Walter Bibikow/Taxi), 11 (altrendo nature/Altrendo), 13 (Andreas Einsiedel/Dorling Kindersley), 16 (Ted Spiegel/National Geographic), 18 (Daniel J. Cox/Photographer's Choice), 19 (Eastcott Momatiuk/The Image Bank), 20 (Walter Bibikow/Taxi), 21 (David W. Hamilton/The Image Bank), 22 (Michel Tcherevkoff/The Image Bank), 23 (James P. Blair/National Geographic), 24 (Andre Gallant/The Image Bank), 25 (David Noton/The Image Bank), 28 (Joe Raedle/Reportage), 29T (Photodisc Collection/Photodisc Blue), 29B (GSO Images/The Image Bank), 30 (Andre Gallant/The Image Bank), 31L (Bloom Productions/Digital Vision), 31R (Philippe Colombi/Photodisc Green), 32 (Andre Gallant/The Image Bank), 33 (Burke/Triolo Productions/Brand X Pictures), 35 (Kelly Kalhoefer/Botanica), 36 (John Giustina/Taxi), 37T (John Warden/Stone), 37B (Ken Graham/Stone), 38 (Walter Bibikow/Taxi), 39 (Joel Sartore/National Geographic), 40 (James P. Blair/National Geographic), 42 (Nancy Simmerman/Stone), 43TL (Getty Images/Taxi), 43TR (Nicholas Veasey/Photographer's Choice), 43ML (Tom Schierlitz/The Image Bank), 43MR (Bill Greenblatt/Liaison), 43BL (Maria Stenzel/National Geographic), 43BR (Bryce Flynn Photography Inc/Taxi), 44L (Stockdisc/Stockdisc Classic), 44M (Ryan McVay/Photodisc Green), 44R (C Squared Studios/Photodisc Green), 45L (Tom Schierlitz/The Image Bank), 45R (Stockdisc/Stockdisc Classic);
Photos.com: pages 15, 34T, 34BL, 34BR.

Substantive Editor
Arlene Worsley

Copy Editors
Frances Purslow
Janice L. Redlin

Designer
Terry Paulhus

Layout
Kathryn Livingstone
Gregg Muller

Photo Researchers
Annalise Bekkering
Jennifer Hurtig

We acknowledge the financial support of the Government of Canada through the Book Publishing Industry Development Program (BPIDP) for our publishing activities.

CONTENTS

The Regions of Canada

Canada is the second largest country on Earth. It occupies an enormous area of land on the North American continent. Studying geography helps draw attention to the seven diverse Canadian regions, including their land, climate, vegetation, and wildlife. Learning about geography also helps in understanding the people in each region, their history, and their culture. The word "geography" comes from Greek and means "earth description."

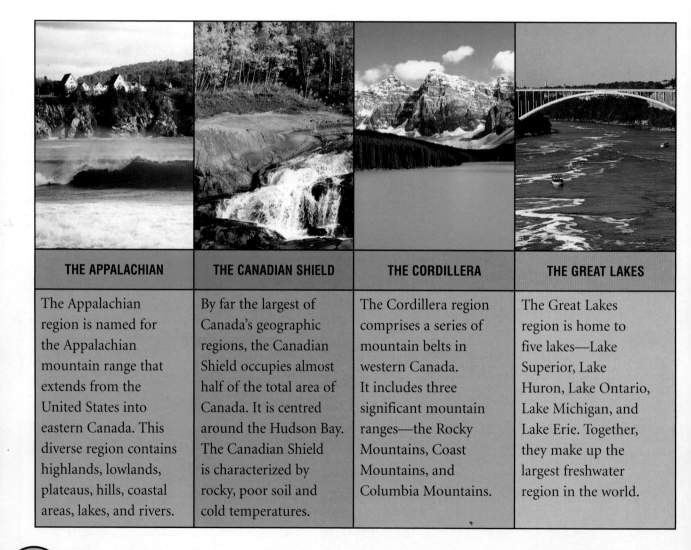

THE APPALACHIAN	THE CANADIAN SHIELD	THE CORDILLERA	THE GREAT LAKES
The Appalachian region is named for the Appalachian mountain range that extends from the United States into eastern Canada. This diverse region contains highlands, lowlands, plateaus, hills, coastal areas, lakes, and rivers.	By far the largest of Canada's geographic regions, the Canadian Shield occupies almost half of the total area of Canada. It is centred around the Hudson Bay. The Canadian Shield is characterized by rocky, poor soil and cold temperatures.	The Cordillera region comprises a series of mountain belts in western Canada. It includes three significant mountain ranges—the Rocky Mountains, Coast Mountains, and Columbia Mountains.	The Great Lakes region is home to five lakes—Lake Superior, Lake Huron, Lake Ontario, Lake Michigan, and Lake Erie. Together, they make up the largest freshwater region in the world.

Canada is home to a variety of landforms. The country hosts sweeping Arctic **tundra**, fertile lowlands, rolling plains, majestic mountains, and vast forests. Each region has a wide range of plants, animals, natural resources, industries, and people.

THE INTERIOR PLAINS	THE NORTH	THE ST. LAWRENCE LOWLANDS
The rolling, low-lying landscape of the Interior Plains is the primary centre for agriculture in Canada. The Interior Plains region lies between the Cordillera and the Canadian Shield.	Much of the North region is composed of thousands of islands north of the Canadian mainland. Distinctive landforms in the region include Arctic lowlands and polar deserts. Glacier mountains are also a recognizable feature in the North.	The St. Lawrence Lowlands region is located on fertile soil surrounding the St. Lawrence River. The region contains a waterway system linking Canada and the United States to the Atlantic Ocean.

The Majestic Appalachian

Mountains, highlands, and plateaus mark the Appalachian region in Canada. The area is an extension of the Appalachian Mountains in the United States. The mountain system covers 2,400 kilometres north to south from Alabama to the Gaspé Peninsula. In Canada, the region also includes the highlands of Newfoundland and Labrador.

The Appalachian region is important to the history, culture, agriculture, and industry of Canada. The first European explorers to reach Canada's shores anchored their ships on the harbours of Newfoundland, Labrador, and the Gaspé Peninsula. They met the Mi'kmaq and Malecite First Nations Peoples. The explorers settled among these groups, bringing their own culture and traditions to the region.

> ❝The first explorers from Europe to reach Canada landed on the shores of the Appalachian region. ❞

Briar Island is the westernmost point in Nova Scotia. Whales are a common sight off the coast in the summer.

The Appalachian region includes the Gaspé Peninsula in Quebec and most of the Atlantic provinces. The eastern provinces of New Brunswick, Nova Scotia, Prince Edward Island, and Newfoundland and Labrador make up the Atlantic provinces.

The Appalachian region has long been important to industry and trade in Canada. Iron, zinc, and gold are mined in the region's mountains. The waters surrounding the Appalachian are rich in fish, including cod, halibut, herring, and

Prince Edward Island rests on a bed of soft, red sandstone, which results in red soil being found throughout the province. The red colour is due to high rust content in the soil.

sole. People in Canada and many parts of the world depend on the region's fishing industry.

The Appalachian soil supports a strong agricultural industry. Crops, such as potatoes and oats, are grown in abundance. Cattle are raised in the Appalachian region and shipped to destinations across North America.

The region boasts busy cities and an active seashore, as well as large stretches of untouched wilderness. Hundreds of species of plants and animals inhabit the Appalachian.

Trees such as maple grow in the fertile lowlands, while spruce trees grow in the Appalachian's thick forests. At least 200 species of birds are found in the region. Also inhabiting Appalachian forests and mountainous areas are hundreds of mammals, such as caribou, moose, bears, coyotes, and beavers.

QUICK FACTS

- The Appalachian region is known for its plentiful growth of potatoes and blueberries.
- Moose are the largest and most common animal in the Appalachian region.

Map of Canadian Geographic Regions

This map of Canada shows the seven geographic regions that make up the country. The regions are divided by their topography, from towering mountains to river valleys, and from Arctic tundra to rolling prairies. Canadian geographic regions are some of the most diverse anywhere in the world.

Studying a map of Canada's geographic regions helps develop an understanding of them, and about the nation as a whole.

LEGEND

- The Appalachian
- The Canadian Shield
- The Cordillera
- The Great Lakes
- The Interior Plains
- The North
- The St. Lawrence Lowlands

Latitude and Longitude

Longitude measures the distance from a spot on the map to an imaginary line called the prime meridian that runs around the globe from the North Pole to the South Pole.

Latitude measures the distance from a spot on the map to an imaginary line called the equator that runs around the middle of the globe.

ARCTIC
OCEAN

GREENLAND

ICELAND

Resolute

Baffin Bay

Great Bear
Lake

THWEST TERRITORIES

Yellowknife

Great Slave Lake

N U N A V U T

Iqaluit

Hudson Strait

TA

Lake Athabasca

Churchill

Hudson Bay

Ungava
Bay

Labrador Sea

SASKATCHEWAN

MANITOBA

Lake
Winnipeg

LABRADOR

iton

Saskatoon

St. John's

Regina

O N T A R I O

Lake Nipigon

Q U E B E C

NEWFOUNDLAND

Winnipeg

Thunder Bay

L. Superior

Sudbury

L. Huron

Quebec

Trois-Rivières

Montreal

Ottawa

L. Michigan

Toronto

L. Ontario

Gulf of
St. Lawrence

PRINCE
EDWARD
ISLAND

NEW
BRUNSWICK

Fredericton

NOVA
SCOTIA

Halifax

ATLANTIC
OCEAN

UNITED STATES

L. Erie

The Map Scale

A map scale is a type of formula. The scale helps determine how to calculate distances between places on a map.

0   500 Kilometres

The Compass Rose

North is indicated on the map by the compass rose. As well, the cardinal directions—north, south, east, and west—and the intermediate directions—northeast, southeast, northwest, southwest—are shown.

N
W   E
S

Earth's Shared History

The Appalachian is not the only geographic area in the world that has highlands, low mountains, and plains spreading toward an ocean. Many scientists believe that the geographic history of Earth and regions around the world share a variety of characteristics.

The Story of Pangaea

The reason Earth has similar regions in different countries is that the world was once made up of one continent that German meteorologist and geologist Alfred Wegener called Pangaea. In 1912, Wegener proposed the theory of continental drift. He theorized that all the land on Earth was part of one large landmass. Pangaea covered nearly half of Earth's surface and was surrounded by an ocean called Panthalassa. Between 245 and 208 million years ago, Pangaea began to split. The pieces of the larger landmass moved apart until they formed seven continents—Africa, Antarctica, Asia, Australia, Europe, North America, and South America.

PERMIAN
225 million years ago

TRIASSIC
200 million years ago

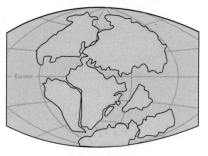

JURASSIC
135 million years ago

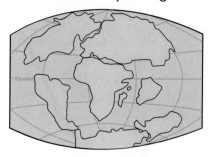

CRETACEOUS
65 million years ago

Arctic and Cordilleran plants can be found in Cape Breton, Nova Scotia. Their presence indicates that some areas in the Appalachian region may have been ice-free during the last glaciation.

Similar soil, landforms, plants, and animals may have been carried to various parts of the world when Pangaea split. Scientists have found fossils in Australia that were from polar climates on northern continents, such as Asia and North America.

How Pangaea Formed the Appalachian

Many of the world's mountain ranges began forming when Pangaea split. Presently, mountains crisscross every continent on the planet. Canada is home to two significant mountain ranges—the Appalachians on the east coast, and the Rocky Mountains in the west.

The Appalachian Mountains, from which this region takes its name, begin in Virginia. This ancient range of hills and mountains has many parts and many names. Located in the Appalachians are the Blue Ridge, the Unaka, and the Cumberland, all of which spread out to the American mid-Atlantic and South. In Canada, the Shickshocks and Notre Dame ranges are located in Quebec, while the Long Range Mountains are found in Newfoundland and Labrador.

QUICK FACTS

- Pangaea comes from a Greek word that means "all earth."

- The Appalachian Mountains were named after a First Nations group that lived in the region when the first Europeans arrived in North America.

- Before Pangaea split, the Appalachian region was part of what is now the Highlands in Scotland and the Atlas Mountains in Africa, which run through Morocco, Algeria, and Tunisia.

Millions of Years Ago

The Appalachian system is made up of some of the oldest mountain ranges on Earth. Some of the mountains began to form billions of years ago, long before plants, animals, and people inhabited the region.

Geologists have found evidence of volcanic activity in the region that may have occurred between 1.1 billion and 540 million years ago. During this period, called the Precambrian era, volcanoes erupted and covered part of the land in molten lava.

> 66 Below the surface of Earth are located massive plates, or enormous chunks of rock that are in constant motion. 99

Over time, these layers of lava compressed and became the marble, slate, and granite that make up "Old" Appalachia. This section of the range runs from Canada through part of New England in the United States. "New" Appalachia is made up of shale, sandstone, and coal created during the Paleozoic era, which began 286 million years ago. This region includes the area west of the Great Valley and the Alleghenies. Both areas range through numerous eastern states.

As a glacier moves over a surface, material from the land is picked up by the glacier and held in the ice as it scrapes over the surface of the land. A glacier can carry rocks that are hundreds of metres in diameter.

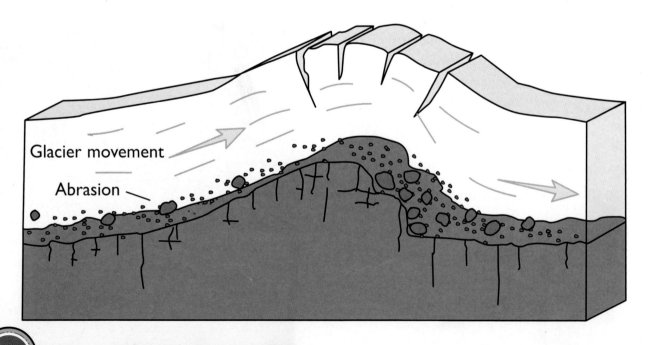

Glacier movement

Abrasion

Shifting Plates

Below the surface of Earth are located massive plates, or enormous chunks of rock. These plates are in constant motion because they rest above a layer of hot, liquid rock. When these plates collide, compressed rocks shoot up to the surface and form majestic mountains, such as the Appalachian mountain range.

Why the Appalachians are Lower

The Appalachian region has many mountain ranges, but they are not the tallest mountains in Canada. The Rocky Mountains, which rise as high as 3,954 metres in western Canada, are taller than the average 914 metres found in the Appalachian area. There are two reasons for the height difference. First, the Applachians are tens of thousands of years older than the Rockies. They have been **eroding** for many years more than the Rockies. The second reason is because of a series of **ice ages** in Earth's distant past. During the last Ice Age, which ended nearly 10,000 years ago, **glaciers** moved south over the Applachian mountain system, pushing the mountains down and wearing away their tall peaks.

WHAT CAN WE LEARN FROM FOSSILS?

Fossils, which are dead plants or animals preserved in rock, give clues to what this region was like millions of years ago. In Newfoundland and Labrador, **archaeologists** have found fossils of one of the oldest-known creatures ever discovered. These creatures, with characteristics of both plant and animal, lived on the bottom of the ocean nearly 600 million years ago. They have yet to be identified.

In Cape Breton and Nova Scotia, scientists have found the fossils of enormous ferns that could only have lived in hot climates. The discovery of these fossils proves that, about 300 million years ago, the Appalachian region was covered in hot, humid rain forests. Today, rain forests are found mainly in the southern hemisphere, in countries with much hotter temperatures than found in the Canada.

Dinosaurs also roamed through the region. Nova Scotia is well known for its fossils from the Triassic and Jurassic periods from 250 and 144 million years ago.

The First Inhabitants

The indigenous peoples of Canada were the first people to live on this land. According to the traditional stories of many indigenous peoples, they have lived in North America for as long as anyone can remember. Scientists have found evidence of human activity in the Appalachian that dates back thousands of years.

Various First Nations groups were living in the Appalachian long before Europeans arrived to explore its shores. They lived off the land by hunting, fishing, and growing crops such as corn, beans, and squash.

The first-known groups in the Appalachian region included the Mi'kmaqs, the Beothuk, and the Passamaquoddy. The Mi'kmaqs lived in Nova Scotia, Prince Edward Island, and parts of New Brunswick. The Passamaquoddy settled in New Brunswick, while the Beothuk settled in Newfoundland and Labrador. Some of these groups were **nomadic**. In winter, they moved inland and lived off food they had grown and hunted. In summer, they moved closer to the coast to catch seafood in the ocean's rich waters.

Some First Nations groups, such as the Beothuk, even hunted whales. First Nations Peoples in this region, as well as the Inuit farther north and the Nootka on the west coast, used all the whale parts for survival.

Uses of the Whale

A **Meat:** Whale meat was a vital source of food for the Nootka Peoples in the Cordillera.

B **Skin and bones:** Some groups have traditionally used whale bones to make elaborate carvings.

C **Blubber, or fat:** The Inuit of Canada's north burn whale blubber for heat and light.

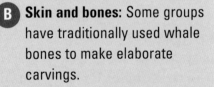

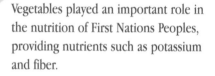

Vegetables played an important role in the nutrition of First Nations Peoples, providing nutrients such as potassium and fiber.

The group that became the largest and most powerful was the Algonquin. The Algonquin were part of a larger group called the Anishinabee, which included the Odawa and Ojibwe peoples who lived in Quebec, Ontario, and Manitoba.

The Malecite live in New Brunswick near the Quebec border. They live with the Mi'kmaq, Passamaquoddy, and Penobscot peoples, who reside in Maine today.

HOW DO WE HONOUR THE FIRST NATIONS PEOPLES OF THE APPALACHIAN?

First Nations culture is fundamental to our Canadian heritage. To celebrate the heritage of the Appalachian region's First Nations Peoples, the government of Nova Scotia declared the month of October Mi'kmaqs History Month. In school, students learn about the province's earliest peoples. Throughout the province, celebrations and festivals are held featuring the traditional culture, foods, and history of the Mi'kmaq people.

Place names are another way to honour the importance of First Nations cultures in the region. Many of the place names in New Brunswick come from Malecite words. Examples of Malecite place names in New Brunswick are Cobscook, Wolastook, and Keswick.

Other names in the region also derive from Mi'kmaq words. Baddeck, Nova Scotia, for example, comes from the Mi'kmaq word "petekook," which means "the place that lies on the backward turn." The word refers to a traditional Mi'kmaq travel route on the river from Bras d'Or Lake.

Arrival from Europe

Beginning around 1000 AD, explorers from Europe arrived to examine Canada's eastern coast. The first-known explorer of the area that would become Canada was a Viking named Leif Ericsson. Ericsson described two locations that he called Markland and Vinland. European exploration of North America began again in the 1500s, when explorers arrived to search for a way to cross the continent and find a faster route to China and India in Asia.

In 1497, John Cabot, an Italian explorer who sailed on behalf of Great Britain, landed on Newfoundland and Labrador. Other explorers followed and built settlements along the coast in the area now called the Grand Banks.

> **"** The success of the fur trade encouraged other explorers to come to Canada. **"**

Viking ships were designed with streamlined hulls and shallow keels, allowing the ship to skim the surface of the water. The design of the ships allowed the Vikings to sail thousands of kilometres from their homes in Scandinavia.

The French also began to arrive in the early 1500s. On his second trip to North America, Jacques Cartier discovered the St. Lawrence River. He built a fort on the banks of a river in a spot the First Nations Peoples called Quebec, which means "the place where the river narrows." During this voyage, Cartier travelled to what is now known as "Mont Réal," or Mount Royal. Mount Royal is one of the main mountains in the Appalachian mountain chain.

In 1608, Samuel de Champlain established a small settlement on the site of Cartier's earlier fort. The settlers eventually traded with neighbouring First Nations Peoples. They traded beaver furs, which were very popular in Europe for making hats, coats, and other items.

The success of the fur trade encouraged other explorers to come to Canada. In 1610, Baron de Poutrincourt, a French colonist, established a settlement called Acadia in Nova Scotia.

QUICK FACTS

▸ Montreal, the largest city in Quebec, was once a Huron village called Hochelaga. It was founded by Jacques Cartier in 1535.

▸ Early fur traders were called *coureurs de bois*, which means "runners of the woods." They were skilled in living in the woods, hunting, and canoeing. The coureurs de bois established settlements throughout eastern Canada.

▸ The Hudson's Bay Company, established in 1670 by King Charles II of Great Britain to compete with the French fur trade, is still a business today.

Legends from the Appalachian

THE MI'KMAQ SISTERS WHO MARRIED STAR HUSBANDS

The ancient story of the Mi'kmaq sisters is very important to the Mi'kmaq people of Nova Scotia. You can see the story told here in very old rock carvings at Kejimkujik Lake in Nova Scotia.

Early one morning, two Mi'kmaq sisters decided to venture into the forest. When night arrived, the two sisters looked up at the stars.

As they looked at the stars, the sisters talked about what it would be like to marry the stars. Soon, the sisters fell asleep. When they awoke in the morning, they discovered that they had been transported. They were greeted by two men who looked like the stars the sisters looked at the night before. The two men said they would go into the forest and get something to eat.

"While we are gone, there is only one thing you must not do. Do not move that flat rock near the tent," the men said.

The sisters agreed, and the men departed for many days. The younger sister decided to move the rock, despite her sister's warnings.

The younger sister looked beneath the rock and began to scream. "Look, sister," she said. "We are above the world and above the sky!" The older sister looked down through the hole and saw that her sister was right. Through the hole, she could see the sky and the forest where they had just been.

The two sisters realized they had been taken far away from their home. They cried and cried until their star husbands returned.

The star husbands agreed to let the sisters return home, giving them rules to follow for the journey. The younger sister broke the rules. Though they were indeed sent home, the sisters were trapped in the tallest tree in the forest, where people believe they still live today.

GLOOSKAP AND MALSUM

The Algonquins are an important First Nations group whose territory traditionally includes part of the Appalachian. This is a traditional Algonquin story about a feud between brothers.

The great Earth Mother had twin sons, Glooskap and Malsum. They were alike in every way, except that Glooskap was good and Malsum was evil.

Each brother had a secret. They each had one great weakness. One day, Malsum asked his brother to share their secrets.

Glooksap knew his brother had evil in his heart, so he lied and told Malsum that his only weakness was a blow from an owl feather. Thinking his brother had revealed his secret, Malsum told Glooskap that his only weakness was a fern root.

Several days later, Malsum struck his brother with an owl feather as Glooskap slept. Glooksap woke up and told his brother that a feather could not harm him!

Angry with his brother, Glooksap went to the side of a pond to think.

While he sat there, he spoke to himself out loud. The beaver was hiding in the grass and heard his secret.

The beaver agreed to tell Malsum the secret if he would give him whatever he wanted. Malsum agreed, but then did not give the beaver what he wanted.

This angered the beaver, so he returned to Glooskap to tell him what had happened. Glooskap realized that his brother only wished him harm, so he picked a fern root and set off to find Malsum. He struck him with the fern root.

Even after his death, Malsum continued his wicked ways. His spirit went underground and turned into a wolf spirit. He still roams the land today, causing mischief.

Mighty Mountains, Tall Peaks

M ost of the Appalachian region is covered by mountain ranges and highlands. These geographical features were once tall mountains but were worn down by glaciers during the last Ice Age.

The Notre Dame Mountains are the longest and tallest mountain range in the Appalachian region. They stretch more than 800 kilometres from the Green Mountains in Vermont to the Gaspé Peninsula in Quebec and New Brunswick. The tallest peak in the mountain range is Mont Jacques Cartier, which is 1,268 metres tall.

" Nova Scotia's tallest peak is White Hill. White Hill rises 532 m above the Nova Scotia highlands. "

Mount Carleton

Mount Carleton, which is 817 metres tall, is the highest peak in the Maritime provinces. Technically, it is not a mountain, but a monadnock. Monadnocks are tall, isolated hills made of hard rock that is not easily eroded. Rock around Mount Carleton eroded from the effects of the last Ice Age, but the peak remained.

Cabot Trail is a 300 kilometre-long road that winds its way along the mountains and highlands in Cape Breton. It offers visitors a spectacular view of the Gulf of St. Lawrence.

Long Range Mountains

The Long Range Mountains, part of the Newfoundland Mountains, stretch along Newfoundland's western shore. The 400-kilometre long mountain range is heavily forested and important to the region's logging industry. In the southern section of the range, near Mont Jacques Cartier, the mountains form a funnel, or passageway, that carries violent winds into the mainland from the Atlantic Ocean. These winds can reach speeds of up to 193 kilometres per hour.

White Hill

Nova Scotia's tallest peak is White Hill. White Hill rises 532 metres above the Nova Scotia highlands. The peak is surrounded by low shrubs and grasses, with few trees. White Hill is located in the northeastern part of Nova Scotia.

Forming Highlands

Mountains are not the only raised landform found in the Appalachian. Steep cliffs border many of the coasts, and sandy beaches can be found on others. Lakes and rivers were also carved out over millions of years. **Fjords** and giant rock formations serve as a reminder of what the region was like millions of years ago.

Labrador boasts gently sloping plateaus, rugged coastlines, and a variety of bays, fjords, and cliffs that range from 60 to 120 metres in height.

QUICK FACTS

- The Shickshock Mountains are nicknamed the "backbone of the Gaspé Peninsula." This is because they run along the south shore of the St. Lawrence River and form a national barrier between the peninsula and the United States.

- Mont Jacques Cartier is also called "Tabletop Mountain" because its summit, or peak, is flat. The peak was worn flat 10,000 years ago when the last Ice Age ended and glaciers moved across Canada and eroded the land.

More Than Just Mountains

The Appalachian region is made up of a variety of landforms. Some landforms include highlands, lowlands, coastal land, lakes, and rivers.

Highlands

New Brunswick, Nova Scotia, Newfoundland, and parts of Quebec are covered in large highland areas. These areas were once part of the Appalachian mountain system, but were eroded over time. These highland, or upland, regions are also called dissected **plateaus**. Dissected plateaus differ from mountains because they are low. They are also different from plateaus because they were formed in the same way as the mountains of the region. Volcanic eruptions, large upheavals under the earth, and collisions with other continents pushed these highland areas up above sea level.

Lowlands

Lowland regions were formed by erosion and glaciers. When the glaciers moved over the soil, they carved out plains and valleys. The fertile soil of these lowland regions makes for good farming.

Lowlands are located on all the islands in this region. The lowlands of New Brunswick, for example, are covered in sandy areas. Water does not drain from this area because it is lower than other parts of the province. So, New Brunswick's lowland area has many lakes, rivers, and swamps.

The Appalachian region has a mixture of forested highlands, fertile lowlands, and expansive coastlines.

Coasts

Coastline almost entirely surrounds the Appalachian region. This is because it includes three major islands, hundreds of smaller islands, and the shores of New Brunswick and the Gaspé Peninsula in Quebec. One of the most spectacular coastlines in the region is the Bay of Fundy in New Brunswick. Large, powerful tides crash along the 150-kilometre long coast of the Bay of Fundy. Prince Edward Island's coasts are much different, with white sand beaches and gently rolling dunes. Nova Scotia's coastline is surrounded by many bays and harbours.

Lakes and Rivers

Lakes are found mainly in the lowland areas of the Appalachian region. Deep indents carved out by the movement of glaciers trapped water in these lakes. Bras d'Or, which is 1,098 square kilometres in surface area, is connected to the Atlantic Ocean. Bras d'Or is a tidal lake because salt water from the sea drains into it. The lake contains both salt water and fresh water, so it is home to creatures that would normally live in one or the other habitat. Saltwater oysters live alongside freshwater rainbow trout.

WHAT ARE FLOWERPOT ROCKS?

Scattered along the coast of the Bay of Fundy are enormous rock formations that stand more than 15 metres tall. Water once covered these formations, called the Hopewell Rocks, and over time they were worn away by the ocean tides. When the coastline became lower, these rocks stood high above the beach. Powerful waves eroding the bottoms of the formations have shaped them into upside-down cones, or flowerpots.

The Ocean Makes the Climate

Different regions and ecosystems not only have diverse landforms, wildlife, and locations, they also have different climates. Climate is the general state of the weather in a region over time. Geography influences climate. Regions near water tend to be wetter. Regions near mountains are often drier because the mountains shield the areas from rain gathered over nearby bodies of water.

The Appalachian region has a coastal climate. Its winters are warmer, and its summers are cooler than inland regions. The climate of the region is influenced by storms that blow in from the Atlantic Ocean.

> " The Appalachian region has a coastal climate with warmer winters and cooler summers than inland regions. "

New Brunswick has the most snow of all three Maritime provinces. Northwest New Brunswick receives 300 to 400 centimetres of snow every year.

The Appalachian region has a wide range of fall colours in September. Hardwood trees such as birches, hickory, sugar maples, and red maples contribute to this colourful landscape.

Winter

Cold winds blowing off the Atlantic Ocean bring storms, snow, and freezing rain to the Appalachian region in winter. Average snowfall in winter is about 55 centimetres. Some parts of the region have seen as much as 100 centimetres in a day.

Spring

Spring temperatures range from below 0° to 14° Celsius. The region receives a large amount of rain in spring, with an average of 65 centimetres during the season.

Summer

Summer temperatures vary widely throughout the region, depending on whether they are on the coast or inland. Average summer temperature highs are about 18° Celsius.

Fall

Fall is the rainiest and foggiest season in the Appalachian region. During the fall season, rainfall averages are between 90 and 120 millimetres. Temperatures drop in the fall, but not as dramatically as in other parts of Canada.

QUICK FACTS

- Nova Scotia's long coastline and its position on the Atlantic Ocean make it one of the foggiest places in Canada, with an average of 122 foggy days each year.

- St. John's, in Newfoundland and Labrador, is Canada's windiest and foggiest city. It receives 124 days of fog, 359 millimetres of precipitation, and average winds of 23.4 kilometres per hour.

Charting the Climate

A region's climate can indicate what it is like to live there. Temperature, snowfall, and even growing seasons are all part of climate.

Information is collected when studying a region's climate. The maps and charts on these pages help describe this information in a visual way.

Average Temperature

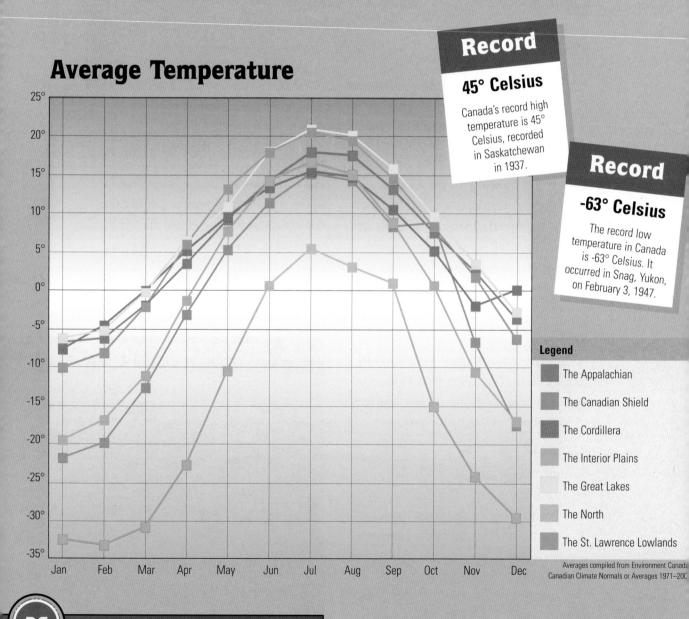

Record

45° Celsius

Canada's record high temperature is 45° Celsius, recorded in Saskatchewan in 1937.

Record

-63° Celsius

The record low temperature in Canada is -63° Celsius. It occurred in Snag, Yukon, on February 3, 1947.

Legend

- The Appalachian
- The Canadian Shield
- The Cordillera
- The Interior Plains
- The Great Lakes
- The North
- The St. Lawrence Lowlands

Averages compiled from Environment Canada Canadian Climate Normals or Averages 1971–200

Average Snowfall

Legend

- over 400 cm
- 300 - 400 cm
- 200 - 300 cm
- 100 - 200 cm
- under 100 cm

Source: Canadian Oxford World Atlas, 4th Edition, 1998

Record

118.1 cm

The record 1-day snowfall, on January 17, 1974, was 118.1 centimetres at Lakelse Lake, British Columbia.

Growing Season

Legend

Average number of days with a median temperature over 5° C

- under 60
- 60 - 100
- 100 - 140
- 140 - 180
- 180 - 220
- 220 - 260
- over 260

Source: Canadian Oxford World Atlas, 4th Edition, 1998

Hurricane Juan Hits Canada

In 2003, Nova Scotia experienced one of the worst storms in its history. Hurricane Juan began as a tropical storm near Bermuda, off the east coast of the United States. It hit Nova Scotia on the morning of September 29. The storm landed between Shad Bay and Prospect, bringing winds that blew 185 kilometres per hour. From Nova Scotia, the storm moved northward. It finally settled on Prince Edward Island 2 days later.

Rain and Flooding

The devastating winds brought rain and flooding. Halifax had up to 44 millimetres of rain. Water levels in the Halifax Harbour rose to 290 centimetres above normal, causing damage and flooding to properties on the coast. Heavy winds also brought enormous waves that pounded the coastal region. Waves as high as 19 metres were reported in Halifax during the worst part of the storm.

> **"** Halifax had up to 44 mm of rain, causing damage and flooding to properties on the coast. **"**

A Terrible Toll

The strong winds, driving rain, and high tides of Hurricane Juan caused extensive damage to the properties and homes of the people of Nova Scotia. It blew down trees, caused power outages across the region, and damaged hundreds of homes and businesses. Extensive damage to power poles and lines caused some people in Nova Scotia to be without power for as long as 2 weeks following the storm. The storm also claimed the lives of eight Nova Scotians.

The worst damage from Hurricane Juan occurred in the eye of the hurricane. Entire sections of trees were completely flattened by strong winds.

Hurricane Juan damaged many homes in the Appalachian region.

Retiring the Name

Environment Canada requested that "Juan" no longer be used to name hurricanes as a result of the extensive damage and loss of lives. Naming hurricanes began in 1950 as a way to identify how many of the storms there had been in a year. Each name corresponds to a letter in the alphabet. The World Meteorological Society creates and monitors the lists of hurricane names. Out of respect for the Canadians who lost lives, loved ones, and property, Juan will no longer be used to name a hurricane.

HOW DID HURRICANE JUAN AFFECT THE PEOPLE OF THE APPALACHIAN?

The most tragic loss during Hurricane Juan was the loss of life. Eight people died during the storm. Many more people lost their homes, businesses, vehicles, and other possessions.

Electricity went out during the storm. More than 100,000 people were without power for 2 weeks following the disaster. People could not contact their friends and families, businesses were forced to shut down, and children were kept home from school.

The storm also damaged the environment. Ninety percent of the trees in Halifax's Point Pleasant Park were knocked down or torn from the ground.

Damage to the region was estimated at more than 100 million dollars. Today, not all the damage has been repaired. People in the region continue to work hard to rebuild their homes and to rebuild their lives.

Natural Resources

The people that live in the Appalachian region rely on its natural resources. Agriculture, mining, fishing, and logging are all industries that depend on the region's natural resources.

Agriculture

Growing crops is challenging in the Appalachian region because of poor soil quality. Potatoes are grown widely throughout the region because they grow well in damp or unfertile soil. Strawberries and blueberries are common in the wild. Oats and hay are grown to feed the cattle that are raised for their milk and meat.

66 Many people are working to replant trees in the Appalachian because many of the region's forests have been destroyed. 99

Logging

Early settlers logged the abundant trees that grew in the Appalachian's once dense forests. In New Brunswick, 87 percent of the forested land is used for logging. People are working to replant trees in the Appalachian because many of the region's forests have been cut down.

Mining and Industry

Glaciers uncovered and deposited rich **mineral** resources in the Appalachian. Iron ore is one of the region's most plentiful resources. It is used to make steel, which is manufactured and sold throughout Canada to build vehicles and heavy machinery.

Gold, silver, limestone, and gypsum are also mined in the Appalachian. Gypsum and limestone are used in construction. Off the coast of Labrador, large deposits of

An average Canadian home requires about 47 cubic metres of wood, or a little more than a truckload of wood for construction.

oil and natural gas are also mined. The Hibernia oil field near Newfoundland is the fifth largest oil reserve ever discovered in Canada. Another type of fuel mined in the region is coal, which is mixed with iron ore to make steel.

Fishing

Fishing has been the most important industry in the Appalachian for centuries. The region is the source for the majority of the fish and seafood eaten by Canadians. Cod was once one of the most plentiful catches off the Atlantic Coast, but overfishing has reduced that supply. Today, fishermen catch crab, lobster, and fish, such as salmon, turbot, halibut, and herring.

Canada's Maritime provinces export more than 400 million kilograms of seafood every year.

WHAT IS AQUACULTURE?

To protect fish populations in the wild from overfishing, many people in the Appalachian region have turned to aquaculture, or fish farming. Salmon, steelhead, trout, and mussels are just some of the species raised on fish farms to sustain the industry.

The fish are raised in ponds or pools where they are fed and protected from predators until they are ready to be sold. Other fish are raised on fish farms and then released into the oceans, rivers, and lakes in an attempt to increase the fish population in the wild.

Depleted fish stocks and disputes with other countries over fishing rights have resulted in many people losing their jobs. Today, it is estimated that 14,000 people in Canada work on fish farms.

Appalachian Soil Quality

Soil is very important to the different regions of Canada. In the Appalachian region, it is important to the agricultural industry, people, and wildlife. Soil is made up of many different substances, including rocks, minerals, decomposed plants, and other materials.

Soil is composed of many layers. The deepest layer is called the parent material. This material is usually made up of solid rock on which the other softer layers of soil rest. The layer of soil above the parent layer is called subsoil. Topsoil is the final layer, which is visible when looking at the ground. Topsoil is often greatly affected by rain and other precipitation, as well as by the crops that grow in it.

❝ The Appalachian region has very little fertile soil, mainly because the land is dominated by areas of granite and limestone. ❞

During low tide on the Bay of Fundy mudflats, crustaceans, such as shrimp, provide food for birds.

Podzol

The Appalachian region has very little fertile soil, mainly because it is dominated by rocky mountains and highland areas that are made of granite and limestone. Much of the soil in the region is known as podzol. Podzol is common in humid and mountainous areas. Podzol is also found in the Canadian Shield region and in the humid and coastal areas of the Cordillera.

The gray or brown soil is made up mostly of rock that has eroded from nearby mountain ranges. The soil is high in aluminum and iron, so it is not good for growing most plants. **Coniferous** trees, such as pines and firs, grow well in this soil. Farmers in the region add nutrients to the soil so they can grow crops.

Peat in the Bogs

The lowland areas of the Appalachian have wetlands and bogs. Bogs are formed in shallow pools, some of which were formed by glaciers millions of years ago. In areas where there are few rivers and streams to drain them, water collects in these pools.

Plant matter decomposes in the pools and forms a layer of a substance called peat. Layers of peat continue to build up until the pool is filled. Peat was once harvested and burned to heat people's homes. Today, it is used as a fertilizer. Areas near bogs are more fertile than the soil in the rest of the region. Farmers also use this land to grow crops.

HOW DO PEOPLE MODIFY THE WETLANDS?

Some parts of the Appalachian were once flooded by salt water. The salt in these wetland areas made the land unsuitable for growing crops. People built levees, or small dams, to contain the water in the rivers, to stop the flow of salt water into the rivers, and to irrigate the land surrounding the rivers to help crops grow.

Growing Things

The vast range of mountains in the Appalachian region is home to hundreds of plants and trees. From wildflowers to trees, the plants in this region have found ways to grow despite the rocky landscape, infertile soil, and sometimes treacherous weather conditions.

In the Forest

Trees grow well in the Appalachian region's soil. The forests produce a mixture of coniferous and **deciduous** trees. Coniferous trees, such as pine, spruce, fir, and tamarack, have needles and are green all year long. Tamarack trees can live longer than 200 years and can grow to heights of 30 metres.

> " Maple trees were important to early life in the region. The sap from the trees can be tapped to make delicious maple syrup. "

Deciduous trees, such as maple, birch, beech, ash, elm, cedar, and oak, lose their leaves in the fall. Maple trees can grow in shady forests and many types of soil. Maple trees were also important to early life in the region. The sap from the trees can be tapped, or collected, and boiled to make delicious maple syrup.

Vegetation

Low shrubs and ample grasses grow well in the Appalachian region. Shrubs, such as wintergreen, cling to rocky regions where there is little soil or protection from strong winds and rain. Bracken, a type of fern, also grows well in the region's forests. Cranberries, blueberries, and partridge berries are common, too.

The Appalachian region displays a vast array of vegetation, making it a beautiful region year-round.

Water Plants

Some plants thrive in the watery wetlands of the region. Marsh grasses are common, as well as floating plants such as the white water lily. Water lilies have thick green leaves and large white blossoms. They are anchored to the marsh bottom by a long, thin stem so they can absorb nutrients from the soil below.

Some plants in the wetlands are **carnivorous**, which means they get their nutrients from animals. The pitcher plant, for example, has a colourful flower that looks like a pitcher with a spout. Insects are attracted to the plant, which is coated with a slippery substance. When they land on the plant, they fall into the base of the flower, where they are ingested by the plant.

Beautiful Blossoms

Wildflowers dot the rolling hills and valleys of the Appalachian region. Flowers, such as primroses, wild roses, mayflowers, and violets, colour the landscape in different shades of red, pink, purple, and yellow.

Fiddleheads are named for their resemblance to the spiral end of a fiddle. Their taste is a cross between asparagus, okra, and green beans.

QUICK FACTS

- Nearly 87 percent of New Brunswick is covered with trees, making it the most heavily forested area in the Appalachian.

- Sheephead is a type of shrub that grows in the Appalachian. In spring, the shrubs blossom with brilliant pink flowers.

- The leaves of bracken are called fronds. Before the fronds open, people often pick them to eat. The closed fronds are called fiddleheads.

Cougars, Whales, and Moose

Animals and birds run, leap, climb, and fly over the varying geography of the Appalachian region. Fish, whales, and other creatures live in the lakes, rivers, and Atlantic Ocean off its seacoast.

❝ Moose, which can weigh as much as 725 kilograms, get their name from an Algonquin word that means 'eater of twigs.' **❞**

Swimming in the Waves

The rivers and lakes of the Appalachian region are filled with aquatic life. Trout, pike, bass, and salmon are some of the freshwater fish found there. Salmon live in the ocean until it is time to spawn, or lay and fertilize eggs. Female salmon return to the same place they were hatched to lay their eggs. Some salmon swim more than 3,200 kilometres to reach their spawning ground.

Other fish, such as cod, mackerel, and herring, swim off the Appalachian coasts. Oysters, lobsters, and scallops live in the shallow coastal waters. Seals warm themselves on the shores of the Appalachian region's beaches and cliffs. Offshore, whales and porpoises swim through the waves.

Magnificent Mammals

Mammals are warm-blooded animals, which means their body temperature does not change dramatically with the temperature of their surroundings.

Small mammals, such as rabbits, squirrels, and skunks, dig burrows and build nests in the trunks of trees. Underground burrows can house hundreds of rabbits. Above ground, foxes, cougars, and lynx look for prey. Cougars and lynx once thrived in the region, but were hunted for their fur. Today, cougars and lynx are **endangered** species.

Besides humans, cougars are the most widely distributed mammals in the western hemisphere. Their range stretches from Canada to South America.

Another common large mammal in the region is the moose. Moose get their name from an Algonquin word that means "eater of twigs." Male moose, called bulls, can weigh as much as 725 kilograms. Black bears live in the forests, too. They are omnivorous, which means they eat both meat and plants. Bears eat foods such as berries, fish, acorns, and insects.

Flapping and Flying

Birds live in the forests and mountains of the Appalachian region. Many birds live in the region year-round, including partridges, pheasants, geese, ducks, owls, and woodpeckers.

Others birds, such as sandpipers, plovers, gulls, gannets, murries, and puffins, nest on the coasts during the winter.

The wood duck was hunted nearly to extinction until its hunting season was closed in 1918. Today, there are over 1 million wood ducks in North America.

QUICK FACTS

- Besides the long distances salmon swim to spawn, their journeys to the spawning ground are always upstream against the current of the rivers that flow toward the oceans.

- Polar bears can be found on the northern coast of Labrador. They have thick layers of fat beneath their white fur to help them blend in with their surroundings and keep them warm in winter. Polar bears can weigh as much as 800 kilograms.

- The lynx and snowshoe hare's relationship is dependent upon the abundance of each species. During the winter, the diet of the lynx is 75 percent hare. When hares are scarce, there are fewer lynx.

Global Warming, Rising Water

One of the greatest dangers facing Earth is global warming. Global warming occurs when Earth's atmosphere contains too many **greenhouse gases**, mostly created by machines. These gases become trapped in Earth's atmosphere, along with heat rising from Earth. Then, the temperature rises on the planet's surface.

Some of the first places to be affected by global warming will be coastal areas, such as the Appalachian region's Atlantic coast. This is because polar icecaps at Earth's North and South Poles melt when the temperature increases. The meltwater makes water levels in the oceans and seas rise, which has a negative affect on any of the world's regions that are near water.

Rising water levels cause damage to coastal habitats that are home to fish, shellfish, and birds. Coastal areas also erode faster when water levels increase. In many areas, the coasts protect more fertile land from eroding into the ocean. If the coasts erode further, there will also be fewer places for migratory birds to nest.

Low-lying coasts react very sensitively to climate change.

The Impact on the Region

Global warming has a negative impact on many other aspects of Earth's climate, geography, plants, and animals. In the Appalachian region, global warming threatens to damage the **ecosystem** of the region. Plants and animals that live in the region will lose their **habitats**. People in the Appalachian will suffer because of the loss of natural resources, such as trees and fish damaged by changing climate.

Q **What can people do about the effects of global warming?**

What are the effects?	What are people doing about it?
Water levels are increasing due to melting icecaps. In time, transportation routes may need to change.	The Confederation Bridge, which connects New Brunswick and Nova Scotia, was built at a height that will ensure it is not covered by water if water levels rise in the next 100 years. This will enable transportation of goods and people to continue between the two provinces.
Higher water levels are eroding the cliffs that border the ocean. These cliffs are where migratory birds, such as gulls, gannets, and sandpipers, make their nests.	People are working to build up coastlines with sandbags, rocks, and wire mesh to prevent the coasts from eroding further.
The coastal region, which is home to many species of plants and animals, is threatened by the effects of global warming.	People are building onshore and offshore sanctuaries for animals and birds that will need shelter if the coastal region is destroyed.

Global warming may cause birds to lay their eggs earlier.

View from Above

There are different ways to view a region. Maps and photos, including those from satellites, help to show the region in different ways.

A map is a diagram that shows an area's surface. Maps can demonstrate many details, such as lakes, rivers, borders, towns, and even roads.

Photos can demonstrate what a region looks like close up. In a photo, specific objects, such as buildings, people, and animals, can be seen.

Satellite photos are pictures taken from space. A satellite thousands of metres in the air can show details as small as a car.

Questions:

What information can be obtained from a photo?

How might a map be useful?

What details are indicated on a satellite photo that cannot be seen on a map?

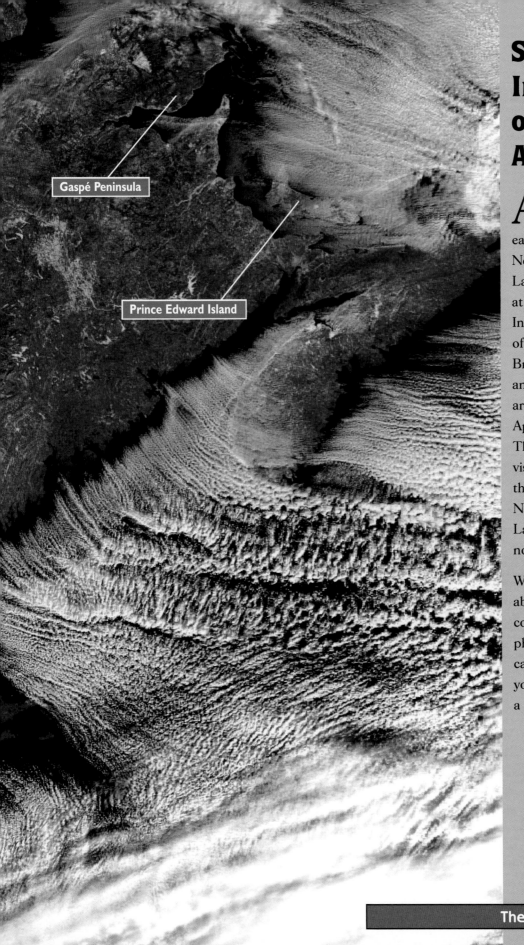

Gaspé Peninsula

Prince Edward Island

Satellite Image of the Appalachian

A weather front is approaching the eastern seaboard of North America. The St. Lawrence River is located at the top left corner. In the top right, the Gulf of St. Lawrence, New Brunswick, Nova Scotia, and Prince Edward Island are shown as part of the Appalachian region. These areas are clearly visible to the north of the main storm clouds. Newfoundland and Labrador, farther to the north, are not shown.

What do you notice about this satellite photo compared to a regular photo? What information can you learn from it that you would not learn from a map?

Technology Tools

People have studied geology for hundreds of years. Geologists study the rocks, earth, and surfaces that make up Earth. Even before the science of geology had a name, ancient peoples studied the rocks and minerals around them. They experimented to find out what kind of rocks were used to make weapons, jewellery, and items they needed in daily life. Flint, a type of rock that is easy to shape and sharpen, was used to make spears. Minerals, such as gold and copper, were too soft to use as weapons or tools and were shaped to make beautiful jewellery.

Today, geologists use some tools that have been around for centuries, as well as more modern tools. These tools range from simple pick hammers to sophisticated computer equipment. Geologists use these tools to study the rocks and minerals they find on land. They study geology in other areas, as well. Modern technology and tools help them study geology under the sea, in volcanoes, and even on the Moon.

Careers in Geology

What are the areas of specialization in geology?

Answer: Geology has many areas of specialization. Some geologists specialize in geological oceanography, which means they study land and rock formations in the oceans. Other geologists specialize in petroleum geology, which means they study areas that may be rich in oil. Other specializations include environmental geology and engineering geology.

Tools of the Trade

Rock hammer or pick:
These special hammers have a flat end that is used to crush larger pieces of rock, and a pointed end, which is used to pick away smaller pieces of rock.

X rays:
X rays help geologists study material in detail. Certain crystals or minerals can be examined very closely by an X ray. Geologists studying ancient fossils or artifacts also use X rays so they can examine delicate objects without damaging them.

Compass:
A compass helps geologists tell which direction they are going. Compasses are very important to geologists, who often work from maps to travel to the areas they are studying.

Seismograph:
A seismograph measures Earth's vibrations. Geologists use seismographs to study the movements of Earth's tectonic plates. Tectonic plates are huge slabs of rock that shift and move beneath Earth's surface. When two or more plates collide, there is an earthquake.

Brushes:
Some of the rocks and materials geologists study are very delicate. Once geologists have uncovered an object in the rock or soil, they use soft brushes to remove dust and debris without causing damage.

Sonar:
Sonar helps geologists map areas that cannot be reached by humans or seen by the human eye. Sonar sends out a beam of sound. Geologists determine what the sonar has hit by the type of vibration that returns. They can map these locations by listening to the sound.

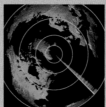

What education is necessary to become a geologist?

Answer: A person can become a geologist after completing a 4-year bachelor of science degree in university. Many people obtain a master's or doctorate degree in geology in order to get more senior positions or to work as professors of geology at the university level.

Mapping Your Library

Maps are important because they show people how to get from place to place. The next time you go to the library, try the following activity.

With a pad and pen, explore the library.

1. How are objects arranged?

2. Are similar books kept in similar places?

3. Is it easier for people to find what they are looking for when items are placed similarly?

Using a grid, make a map of what is kept in each aisle.

4. Are there aisles for special kinds of books? For example, are there sections for books about different countries, different animals, and different plants?

5. What do these sections tell you about the subjects they cover?

When you have finished making your map, think about some of the things you would like to learn more about.

6. Can you find the subjects by looking at your map?

7. Are there any patterns to the way the books are arranged?

8. Have you never borrowed a book from some sections of the library? Try taking a book out from a section of the library you have never explored before.

Navigating Your Birthday

To locate a certain place on Earth, mapmakers came up with the latitude and longitude grid. This grid is a way of dividing Earth into sections using lines that circle Earth from east to west and from north to south.

1. Look at a globe or a map of the world in an atlas.

2. Write down your birthday on a separate piece of paper. Now write the month of your birthday in numbers using the chart below:

January = 1	April = 4	July = 7	October = 10
February =2	May = 5	August = 8	November = 11
March =3	June = 6	September = 9	December = 12

3. Use the month you were born as your latitude and the day you were born as your longitude. Notice that the latitude for your birthday could be north or south of the equator. The longitude for your birthday could be east or west of the prime meridian. For example, if your birthday is September 30, then the coordinates would be 9°N 30°W, 9°N 30°E, 9°S 30°W, and 9°S 30°E.

4. Follow your coordinates on the map. Where on the map does your birthday take you? Find all four locations.

Further Research

Books

Find out more about Canada's regions and landscapes.

Bird, J. B. *The Natural Landscapes of Canada.* Mississauaga, ON: J. Wiley and Sons, 1980.

Learn more about the effects of Hurricane Juan on the Appalachian.

Maher, Stephen. *Hurricane Juan.* Halifax, NS: Nimbus Publishing, 2003.

Web Sites

To learn more about the Appalachian region, its people, and the provinces that are in it, visit:

Encarta Encyclopedia
www.encarta.com

To learn more about the people of Canada and the Appalachian, visit:

Canadian Museum of Civilization
www.civilization.ca

To learn more about the climate of the Appalachian region and the rest of Canada, visit:

Environment Canada Seasonal Forecast
http://weatheroffice.ec.gc.ca/saisons/index_e.html#climatology

Glossary

archaeologists: people who study the past by examining the remains of ancient cultures and civilizations

carnivorous: a type of plant or animal that eats other animals

coniferous: evergreen trees that bear cones

deciduous: trees that lose their leaves in winter

ecosystem: all of the living and nonliving things in a specific area

endangered: threatened with extinction

eroding: wearing away by wind, water, or other elements

fjords: inlets that are nearly surrounded by steep cliffs

glaciers: large, slow-moving chunks of ice

greenhouse gases: atmospheric gases that can reflect heat back to Earth

habitats: places or environments where plants and animals live

ice ages: time periods when Earth was widely covered in ice

mineral: an element, or substance that occurs in nature that is not a plant or animal

nomadic: to travel from place to place, depending on the seasons

plateaus: flat, level areas

tundra: an area in the Far North that is too cold for trees

Index